ALICE'S PIER 21

Author: Maryann Hayatian

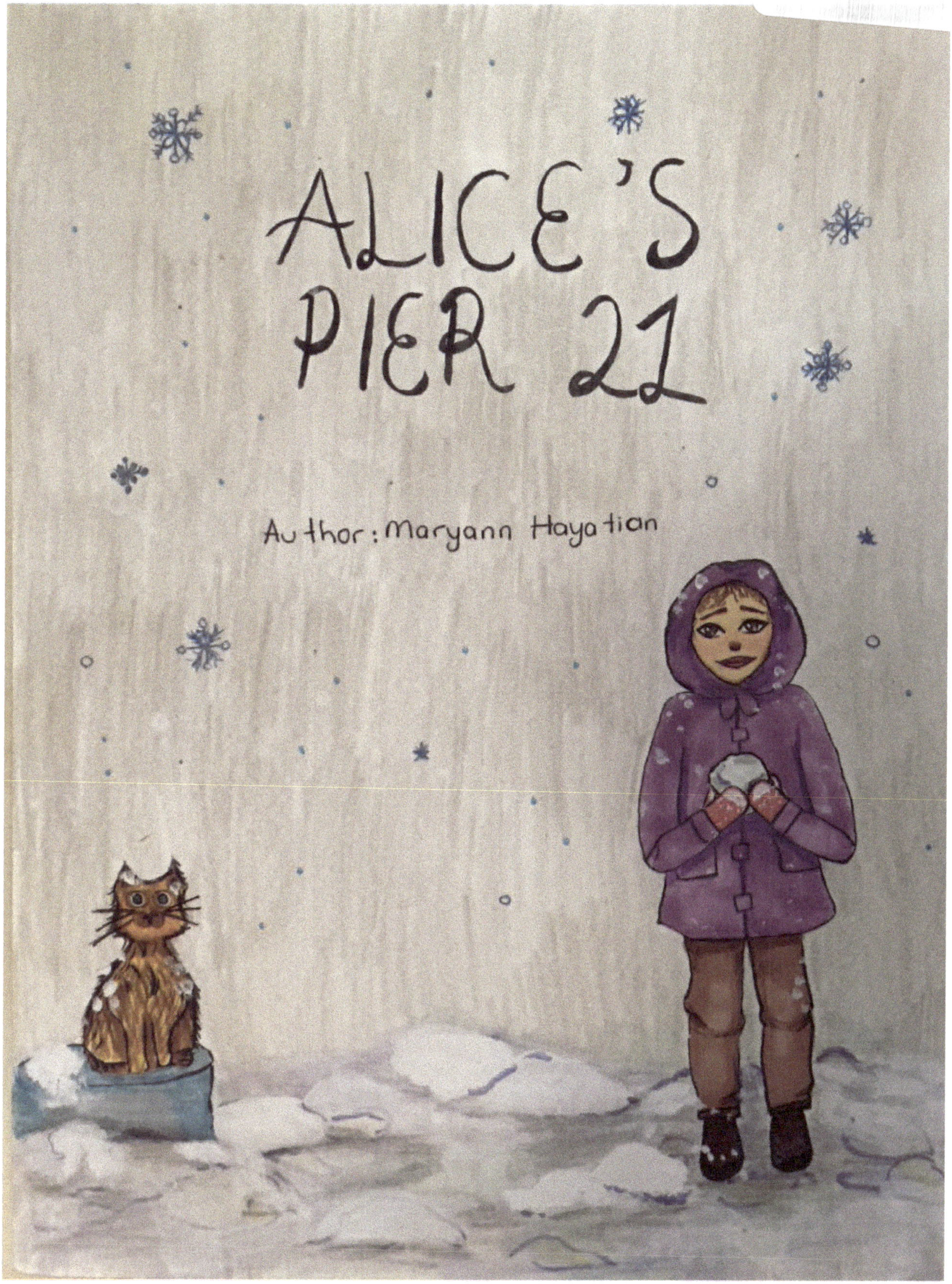

www.butterflyanthology.com

© 2020 MaryAnn Hayatian

ButterflyAnthology

ISBN 978-1-989277-67-6

All rights reserved. No part of this book may be reproduced, stored in a retrieval system or transmitted in any form or by any means without the prior written permission of the publishers, except by a reviewer who may quote brief passages in a review to be printed in a paper or journal.

My mother Alice,

Thanks for your love, nurture, support,

your adorable advices and your bravery.

You are always ready for adventures.

Hello! My name is Alice, I'm eight years old and I reside with my dad, my mom and my big brother Eddie. We recently moved to Canada, and do I have a story to tell you!

It all started in the morning of December 1962. I was busy playing with my toys with Shirley, my doll on my bedroom floor, which I shared this room with Eddie.

"Alice!", my mom yells.

"Yes mom?" I asked and got up from the floor.

"Come to the kitchen, your dad and I have something to discuss. Get dressed first."

What now? I did the dishes already.

I got dressed for the day and walked to the kitchen

Holding Shirley.

Dad, mom and Eddie were already seated at the kitchen table, so I just sat on the extra chair.

So here it goes.

"Your dad and I don't see good opportunities here in Alexandria, Egypt." My mom said.

I smiled because I didn't know what was my mom talking about. Work has ended, we don't have lots money to pay out bills and the education here is unknown. Her dad said.

"We want to apply as residents to be citizens in Canada and if we are accepted, we will move there.

"Canada?!" Eddie yelled.

"Where's that?" I asked.

"It's cold there." Eddie continued.

"Canada is a nice place." My dad is convinced.

"We will apply this month, get our passport and wait for an answer." Mom said.

"Mom, can Shirley come too?" I asked.

"Yes."

I smiled. Wherever I go, Shirley goes.

The next day, we all got dressed up nicely to go get our passport photo taken and filled out the passport application papers. We brought them to the Canadian Consulate the same day, where everything was sent by post.

As we arrived home, with my curiosity, I asked questions about Canada to my parents.

"Where in Canada we will travel?"

"Halifax, Canada." Dad replied.

"There's snow!" Eddie said.

"Where in Canada are we going to stay?"

"Montreal, Canada." dad answered

"Never heard." I said

Eddie laughed.

Two weeks arrived and the immigration papers had been given by the postman.

Dad opened the envelope and took out the papers and passport for his family.

"Alright everyone!" Dad said with a big smile on his face.

As we heard him, we all ran to him.

"We are going to Canada!" He continued.

Mom took the papers to look.

Eddie and I were hugging.

We were very happy, this was our chance.

"How will we get there?" I asked.

"By ship." Mom answered.

"Taking the plane is faster to get there." Dad suggested.

"No ship is fine." Mom made the final decision.

We all started to laugh.

Mom didn't like planes even though she never took one.

"Then we will take 2 ships which will take us 17 days and one train for 24 hours." Dad said

As 1962 was ending, the family started to get ready for their journey to Montreal, Canada.

Eddie and I were eager to finally speak English. No one rarely spoke it here, it was foreign. My parents knew French and there are people who speak French in Canada too. It's good that Eddie and I would read English books and we were taught the basics by a neighbor.

We started packing our suitcases with clothes, toys and belongings we wanted to keep.

January 1963 arrived and we took the first ship called Ausonia at the Alexandria port in Egypt, that took us to Europe. We stopped to Venice, Italy where we stayed there for the night at a hotel and the next day, we took another ship called Vulcania that will travel to different countries non stop until we arrive to Canada.

While we stayed in Venice, Italy, we went to an Italian restaurant. I had my first pizza.

We took walks on the tiny streets of Venice, watching the scenery and people with gondolas getting their rides to their destination.

We went to Saint Mark's square where there is the Basilica, stores and activities.

The next day, we got are suitcases ready and a man from the hotel drove us by car, to the Venice port, where we will take the Vulcania ship.

We were on the passengers list.

VULCANIA 1963 PASSENGER LIST

De Heer P. Von der Aa
De Heer F.A Abena
Mevr F.A Abena
Paher W. Abena
De Heer H.A Alkerboom
Mevr H.A Alkerboom
Mevr. M Arts
De Heer M. Arts
De Heer B. Th. Arts
De Heer J. van das
De Heer Aven
Mevr J. van das Aven
G. Papazian
S. Papazian
E. Papazian
A. Papazian

De Heer D. Bailio
De Heer Th. W von Baikal
Mevr Th. W von Baikal
De Heer P. L. von Ballopolle
Mevr P.L von Ballopolle
Jonpeheer M. von Ballopolle
De Haer P. Bornhoom
Jonpeheer H. V. Barhoom

Mevr. J. van der Berg
Janpujulle F.W van der Berp

De Heer J. Berges
Mej. M. Berkelas
Jonpehos P. H Berkelas
Jonpehos P. A Berkelas
Janpejofir M. Berkelas
De Heer Beyen
Mevr A Beyen
De Heer J. A Boer
Mevr A. Boer
Jonpebeer H. Bopers
Janpejelle M. C Bopers
De Heer W. A.J von Bonnel
De Heer W. Borper
De Heer F. Bow
De Heer J. Bouwers

Mevr A. Bofks
De Heer F. Bornes
De Heer J.F Bonnes
Mevr A.J Bonnes

De Hees H. Bouwers
Mej H. Bouwers
Jonpeber Bouwers
Jonpeber W. A.J Bonnel

Mevr W. K. Birtle

We had elegant dinners on the ship.

There were activities for everyone. I played board games with Eddie.

We had our own room to share with bunk beds.

We had a coach showing us what to do with our life jacket in case of urgency.

There were waves at a distance due to ice interfering the ship's way to the North.

Ship workers had to look out for the coast is clear by cutting the ice.

On January 21, 1963, the ship arrived to Canada at Pier 21 in Halifax, Nova Scotia.

We walked from the ship to the immigration center.

The officer at Pier 21 stamped our passports and gave us checkups, to get us ready for our next voyage with the train.

As we stood outside at the train station, our suitcases were getting loaded on the train.

I was eager to take a ride with the Canadian Pacific train.

The scenery was beautiful. Everything was decorated with snow.

As one day went by, the train stopped at the Montreal Central Station. We got out of the train and took our suitcases. We had to walk up the stairs to our entrance outside.

We rented an apartment on D'Anvers street in Park Extenson. An area in Montreal, Canada.

And at last, I played with the snow!

As the seasons changed. My family and I got to sight see Montreal. First was the Mont Royal mountain. You can see the view of Montreal. We went to the Saint Joseph's oratory, it had a history story to tell and the way it was built with its purpose.

Years later, I still had questions about Canada. I went to sit beside my dad at the living room table, where he would do his work as a jeweler.

"Dad?" I said.

"Yes?" He answered.

"Why did we come to Canada?"

"Because of you, your brother and your mother. Yes, for myself too."

He started laughing.

"Because Canada chose us to set a good example for our nation land."

www.ingramcontent.com/pod-product-compliance
Lightning Source LLC
Chambersburg PA
CBHW061113070526
44583CB00027B/3283